Sourdough Discard Cookbook

40+ Beginner-Friendly Recipes and a 7-Step Starter Guide

mf

copyright © 2024 Mary Golanna

All rights reserved No part of this book may be reproduced, or stored in a retrieval system, or transmitted in any form or by any means, electronic, mechanical, photocopying, recording, or otherwise, without express written permission of the publisher.

Disclaimer

By reading this disclaimer, you are accepting the terms of the disclaimer in full. If you disagree with this disclaimer, please do not read the guide.

All of the content within this guide is provided for informational and educational purposes only, and should not be accepted as independent medical or other professional advice. The author is not a doctor, physician, nurse, mental health provider, or registered nutritionist/dietician. Therefore, using and reading this guide does not establish any form of a physician-patient relationship.

Always consult with a physician or another qualified health provider with any issues or questions you might have regarding any sort of medical condition. Do not ever disregard any qualified professional medical advice or delay seeking that advice because of anything you have read in this guide. The information in this guide is not intended to be any sort of medical advice and should not be used in lieu of any medical advice by a licensed and qualified medical professional.

The information in this guide has been compiled from a variety of known sources. However, the author cannot attest to or guarantee the accuracy of each source and thus should not be held liable for any errors or omissions.

You acknowledge that the publisher of this guide will not be held liable for any loss or damage of any kind incurred as a result of this guide or the reliance on any information provided within this guide. You acknowledge and agree that you assume all risk and responsibility for any action you undertake in response to the information in this guide.

Using this guide does not guarantee any particular result (e.g., weight loss or a cure). By reading this guide, you acknowledge that there are no guarantees to any specific outcome or results you can expect.

All product names, diet plans, or names used in this guide are for identification purposes only and are the property of their respective owners. The use of these names does not imply endorsement. All other trademarks cited herein are the property of their respective owners.

Where applicable, this guide is not intended to be a substitute for the original work of this diet plan and is, at most, a supplement to the original work for this diet plan and never a direct substitute. This guide is a personal expression of the facts of that diet plan.

Where applicable, persons shown in the cover images are stock photography models and the publisher has obtained the rights to use the images through license agreements with third-party stock image companies.

Table of Contents

Introduction 7
What Is Sourdough? 9
    What is Sourdough Discard? 10
    Benefits of Sourdough Discard 11
Sourdough Discard Recipes 13
    Sourdough Discard Pancakes 14
    Sourdough Discard Crackers 15
    Sourdough Discard Muffins 16
    Sourdough Discard Pizza Crust 17
    Sourdough Discard Banana Bread 18
    Sourdough Discard Waffles 19
    Sourdough Discard Flatbread 20
    Sourdough Discard Cinnamon Rolls 21
    Sourdough Discard Biscuits 23
    Sourdough Discard Chocolate Chip Cookies 24
    Sourdough Discard Scones 25
    Sourdough Discard Chocolate Brownies 26
    Sourdough Discard Fritters 27
    Sourdough Discard Pretzels 28
    Sourdough Discard Dumplings 30
    Sourdough Discard Bagels 31
    Sourdough Discard Cornbread 32
    Sourdough Discard Cheese Crackers 33
    Sourdough Discard Lemon Bars 34
    Sourdough Discard Garlic Knots 35
    Sourdough Discard Pancake Bites 36
    Sourdough Discard Oatmeal Cookies 37
    Sourdough Discard Cheese Biscuits 39
    Sourdough Discard Chocolate Muffins 40

Sourdough Discard Tortillas	42
Sourdough Discard Apple Cake	43
Sourdough Discard Pita Bread	45
Sourdough Discard Peanut Butter Cookies	47
Sourdough Discard Blueberry Muffins	49
Sourdough Discard Savory Pancakes	50
Sourdough Discard Chocolate Chip Scones	52
Sourdough Discard Garlic Herb Breadsticks	54
Sourdough Discard Apple Fritters	56
Sourdough Discard Pizza Rolls	58
Sourdough Discard Carrot Cake	60
Sourdough Discard Soft Pretzels	62
Sourdough Discard Snickerdoodles	64
Sourdough Discard Veggie Frittata	66
Sourdough Discard Banana Oat Muffins	68
Sourdough Discard Jalapeño Cornbread	70
Sourdough Discard Rosemary Focaccia	72
7-Step Plan to Get Started with Sourdough Discard	**73**
Step 1: Gather Ingredients and Tools	73
Step 2: Understand Sourdough Discard	76
Step 3: Start with Simple Recipes	78
Step 4: Learn Basic Baking Techniques	81
Step 5: Measure Accurately	84
Step 6: Follow Recipes Carefully	87
Step 7: Experiment and Enjoy	90
Conclusion	**94**
FAQs	**97**
References and Helpful Links	**100**

Introduction

Sourdough baking has captivated the culinary world for centuries, offering a rich history and a depth of flavor that modern baking often lacks. At its core, sourdough is a traditional method of bread-making that relies on wild yeast and lactic acid bacteria, a process that has been cherished since ancient times. This method not only produces a unique tangy taste but also enhances the nutritional value and digestibility of bread.

Central to this ancient art is the sourdough starter, a living culture of flour and water teeming with natural yeast and bacteria. This magical concoction is what gives sourdough its distinctive flavor and texture. However, maintaining a sourdough starter involves periodic feedings, during which a portion of the starter—known as sourdough discard—is removed to keep the culture thriving.

The idea of discarding perfectly good starter might seem wasteful, but that's where creativity comes into play. Sourdough discard is a versatile ingredient that can be transformed into a myriad of delightful recipes, from pancakes and waffles to crackers and cookies.

Not only does this practice minimize waste, but it also opens up a world of culinary possibilities for beginners and seasoned bakers alike.

In this guide, we will talk about the following;

- What is Sourdough?
- What is Sourdough Discard?
- Benefits of Sourdough Discard
- Sample Recipes
- 7-Step Plan to Get Started with Sourdough Discard Recipes

Continue reading to explore 41 easy-to-follow recipes and a step-by-step plan to embark on your sourdough adventure. By the end of this guide, you'll gain a deeper appreciation for the art of sourdough discard baking.

What Is Sourdough?

Sourdough bread is created through a natural fermentation process that utilizes wild yeast and lactic acid bacteria. Unlike traditional bread, which uses commercial yeast, sourdough is made with a starter. This starter is a blend of flour and water that attracts wild yeast from the surroundings.

The roots of sourdough trace back thousands of years to ancient Egypt, making it one of the oldest forms of leavened bread. This traditional method has sustained its cultural significance across various civilizations, from the Gold Rush miners of San Francisco to the rustic bread-baking traditions of Europe.

The magic of sourdough lies in its fermentation process. When flour and water are combined, enzymes in the flour break down starches into sugars. Wild yeast and lactic acid bacteria feed on these sugars, producing carbon dioxide gas and organic acids. The carbon dioxide causes the dough to rise, while the acids contribute to sourdough's tangy flavor and act as natural preservatives.

The benefits of this fermentation extend beyond flavor. The lactic acid bacteria improve the bioavailability of nutrients, making sourdough easier to digest compared to standard bread. This process also lowers the glycemic index of the bread, helping to regulate blood sugar levels. Furthermore, the long fermentation breaks down gluten, which may make sourdough more tolerable for individuals with gluten sensitivities.

What is Sourdough Discard?

Sourdough discard is an integral part of the sourdough baking process, yet it often raises questions among new bakers. Essentially, sourdough discard refers to the portion of the starter that is removed and set aside during each feeding. This removal is necessary to keep the starter healthy and prevent it from growing too large, which would make it unmanageable and deplete its food supply more quickly.

The discard process works like this: when feeding your sourdough starter, you take out a portion of the existing mixture before adding fresh flour and water. This practice ensures that the yeast and bacteria within the starter remain balanced and active, ready to leaven your next loaf of bread. Without this step, the starter can become overly acidic and sluggish, leading to less reliable baking results.

While discarding might seem wasteful, it's actually an opportunity to embrace sustainability in your kitchen.

Sourdough discard is a versatile ingredient that can be used in a variety of recipes, providing a subtle tang and depth of flavor to dishes beyond traditional bread. From pancakes and muffins to crackers and pizza crusts, the possibilities are endless.

By incorporating sourdough discard into your cooking routine, you not only minimize waste but also add a unique twist to everyday recipes. This approach encourages creativity and resourcefulness, making every meal an opportunity to explore new flavors and textures.

Benefits of Sourdough Discard

The sourdough discard process not only benefits your starter but also has numerous advantages for both you and the environment:

1. **Versatility in Cooking**: Sourdough discard is incredibly versatile, easily incorporated into a variety of recipes. It can serve as a base for pancakes, waffles, muffins, pizza crusts, and even crackers, allowing for endless culinary possibilities.

2. **Unique Flavor Enhancement**: The fermentation process of sourdough starter imparts a subtle tang and complexity to dishes. This distinctive flavor can elevate both sweet and savory recipes, turning simple meals into gourmet experiences.

3. **Reduction of Kitchen Waste**: By utilizing sourdough discard, you minimize food waste in your kitchen. Instead of discarding it, you can transform it into delicious creations, contributing to more sustainable cooking practices.

4. **Encouragement of Creativity**: Using sourdough discard encourages experimentation and creativity in the kitchen. It offers home cooks the chance to try new recipes and develop unique variations on classic dishes, enhancing culinary skills.

5. **Promotion of Sustainability**: Incorporating sourdough discard into your cooking aligns with eco-friendly habits. It supports the growing emphasis on reducing food waste and conserving resources, fostering a more sustainable kitchen environment.

Overall, the sourdough discard process not only benefits your starter but also promotes culinary exploration and sustainability in the kitchen.

Sourdough Discard Recipes

Now that you know the benefits of incorporating sourdough discard into your cooking, it's time to put it into practice. Here are a few delicious recipes to get you started:

Sourdough Discard Pancakes

Ingredients:

- 1 cup sourdough discard
- 1 cup all-purpose flour
- 1 tablespoon sugar
- 1 teaspoon baking soda
- 1 teaspoon baking powder
- 1/2 teaspoon salt
- 1 egg
- 1 cup milk
- 2 tablespoons melted butter

Instructions:

1. In a bowl, whisk together the sourdough discard, egg, milk, and melted butter.
2. In another bowl, combine the flour, sugar, baking soda, baking powder, and salt.
3. Gradually incorporate the dry ingredients into the wet mixture, stirring until just combined.
4. Warm a non-stick skillet on medium heat.
5. For each pancake, spoon 1/4 cup of batter onto the skillet. Cook until bubbles form on the top, then turn over and cook until golden brown.
6. Serve with your favorite toppings.

Sourdough Discard Crackers

Ingredients:

- 1 cup sourdough discard
- 1 cup all-purpose flour
- 1/4 cup olive oil
- 1/2 teaspoon salt
- 1/2 teaspoon dried herbs (such as rosemary or thyme)

Instructions:

1. Preheat the oven to 350°F (175°C).
2. Mix the sourdough discard, flour, olive oil, salt, and herbs in a bowl until a dough forms.
3. Roll out the dough on a floured surface to about 1/8-inch thickness.
4. Use a knife or cookie cutter to cut into your preferred shapes.
5. Place on a baking sheet lined with parchment paper and bake for 15-20 minutes until golden brown.
6. Allow to cool before serving.

Sourdough Discard Muffins

Ingredients:

- Sourdough discard, 1 cup
- All-purpose flour, 1 cup
- Sugar, 1/2 cup
- Milk, 1/2 cup
- Vegetable oil, 1/4 cup
- Egg, 1
- Baking soda, 1 tsp
- Salt, 1/2 tsp
- Vanilla extract, 1/2 tsp

Instructions:

1. Set your oven to 375°F (190°C) and prepare a muffin tin by placing paper liners in each cup.
2. In a bowl, mix together the sourdough discard, milk, vegetable oil, egg, and vanilla extract.
3. In a separate bowl, mix together the flour, sugar, baking soda, and salt.
4. Blend the dry ingredients into the wet mixture until they are just incorporated.
5. Spread the batter uniformly into each muffin cup.
6. Bake for 18 to 20 minutes, checking doneness by inserting a toothpick into the center; it should come out clean.

Sourdough Discard Pizza Crust

Ingredients:

- Sourdough discard, 1 cup
- All-purpose flour, 1 1/2 cups
- Warm water, 1/2 cup
- Olive oil, 1 tbsp
- Salt, 1 tsp
- Sugar, 1 tsp
- Instant yeast, 1 tsp

Instructions:

1. In a bowl, mix the warm water, sugar, and yeast, then let it rest for 5 minutes.
2. Incorporate the sourdough discard, olive oil, and salt into the yeast mixture.
3. Slowly mix in the flour until a dough forms, then knead for 5 minutes.
4. Place dough in an oiled bowl, cover, and let rise until doubled in size, about 1 hour.
5. Preheat the oven to 475°F (245°C).
6. Roll out the dough on a floured surface and transfer to a pizza pan.
7. Add your favorite toppings and bake for 12-15 minutes.

Sourdough Discard Banana Bread

Ingredients:

- Sourdough discard, 1 cup
- Ripe bananas, mashed, 1 1/2 cups
- Butter, melted, 1/2 cup
- Sugar, 1 cup
- Eggs, large, 2
- Vanilla extract, 1 teaspoon
- All-purpose flour, 1 1/2 cups
- Baking soda, 1 teaspoon
- Salt, 1/2 teaspoon

Instructions:

1. Preheat the oven to 350°F (175°C) and grease a loaf pan.
2. In a large bowl, mix the melted butter, sugar, eggs, mashed bananas, vanilla, and sourdough discard.
3. In another bowl, whisk together the flour, baking soda, and salt.
4. Mix the dry ingredients with the wet ones until they are just blended.
5. Transfer the batter to the prepared loaf pan and bake for 60-70 minutes, or until a toothpick inserted in the center emerges clean.

Sourdough Discard Waffles

Ingredients:

- Sourdough discard, 1 cup
- All-purpose flour, 1 cup
- Sugar, 1 tablespoon
- Baking powder, 1 teaspoon
- Baking soda, 1/2 teaspoon
- Salt, 1/2 tablespoon
- Egg, 1
- Milk, 1 cup
- Melted butter, 3 tablespoon

Instructions:

1. Preheat your waffle iron.
2. In a bowl, whisk together the sourdough discard, egg, milk, and melted butter.
3. In another bowl, mix the flour, sugar, baking powder, baking soda, and salt.
4. Combine the dry ingredients with the wet ingredients and mix until smooth.
5. Pour the batter into the preheated waffle iron and cook according to the manufacturer's instructions.
6. Serve with syrup or your favorite toppings.

Sourdough Discard Flatbread

Ingredients:

- 1 cup sourdough discard
- 1 cup all-purpose flour
- 2 tablespoons olive oil
- 1/2 teaspoon salt
- 1/2 teaspoon garlic powder

Instructions:

1. In a bowl, mix together the sourdough discard, flour, olive oil, salt, and garlic powder until a dough forms.
2. Divide the dough into small balls and roll out each ball into a thin circle.
3. Heat a skillet over medium heat and lightly grease it.
4. Cook each flatbread for 2-3 minutes on each side until bubbles form and the bread is golden brown.
5. Serve warm with dips or as a wrap.

Sourdough Discard Cinnamon Rolls

Ingredients:

- 1 cup sourdough discard
- 2 cups all-purpose flour
- 1/2 cup warm milk
- 1/4 cup butter, melted
- 1 egg
- 1/4 cup sugar
- 1 teaspoon salt
- 1 teaspoon instant yeast

For filling:

- 1/4 cup butter, softened
- 1/2 cup brown sugar
- 1 tablespoon ground cinnamon

Instructions:

1. Combine milk, sugar, and yeast in a bowl and let it sit for 5 minutes.
2. Add the sourdough discard, melted butter, and egg to the yeast mixture.
3. Gradually add flour and salt, kneading until a soft dough forms.
4. Let the dough rise in an oiled bowl for 1-2 hours or until doubled.

5. Roll out the dough into a rectangle, spread with softened butter, and sprinkle with brown sugar and cinnamon.
6. Roll up the dough and slice into rolls. Place in a greased baking dish.
7. Preheat the oven to 350°F (175°C) and bake for 25-30 minutes.

Sourdough Discard Biscuits

Ingredients:

- 1 cup sourdough discard
- 2 cups all-purpose flour
- 1 tablespoon baking powder
- 1/2 teaspoon baking soda
- 1/2 teaspoon salt
- 1/2 cup cold butter, cubed
- 1/2 cup milk

Instructions:

1. Set the oven to 425°F (220°C).
2. In a bowl, mix the flour, baking powder, baking soda, and salt.
3. Cut in the cold butter until the mixture resembles coarse crumbs.
4. Add the sourdough discard and milk, mixing until a dough forms.
5. Roll out the dough on a floured surface and cut into circles.
6. Place biscuits on a baking sheet and bake for 12-15 minutes.

Sourdough Discard Chocolate Chip Cookies

Ingredients:

- 1 cup sourdough discard
- 1 1/2 cups all-purpose flour
- 1/2 cup butter, softened
- 1/2 cup sugar
- 1/2 cup brown sugar
- 1 egg
- 1 teaspoon vanilla extract
- 1/2 teaspoon baking soda
- 1/4 teaspoon salt
- 1 cup chocolate chips

Instructions:

1. Preheat the oven to 375°F (190°C).
2. In a bowl, cream together the butter and sugars.
3. Mix in the sourdough discard, egg, and vanilla extract.
4. Gradually add in the flour, baking soda, and salt until fully combined.
5. Stir in the chocolate chips.
6. Drop spoonfuls of dough onto a greased baking sheet and bake for 8-10 minutes.
7. Let cool before serving.

Sourdough Discard Scones

Ingredients:

- 1 cup sourdough discard
- 2 cups all-purpose flour
- 1/4 cup sugar
- 1 tablespoon baking powder
- 1/2 teaspoon salt
- 1/2 cup cold unsalted butter, cubed
- 1/2 cup heavy cream
- 1 teaspoon vanilla extract

Instructions:

1. Preheat the oven to 400°F (200°C).
2. In a bowl, mix together the sourdough discard, flour, sugar, baking powder, and salt.
3. Cut in the cold butter until the mixture resembles coarse crumbs.
4. Add in the heavy cream and vanilla extract, mixing until a dough forms.
5. On a floured surface, roll out the dough into a circle about 1-inch thick.
6. Cut the circle into 8 wedges and place on a greased baking sheet.
7. Bake for 15-20 minutes or until golden brown.
8. Let cool before serving with jam or clotted cream.

Sourdough Discard Chocolate Brownies

Ingredients:

- 1 cup sourdough discard
- 1/2 cup unsweetened cocoa powder
- 1 cup sugar
- 1/2 cup melted butter
- 2 large eggs
- 1 tsp. vanilla extract
- 1/2 tsp. salt
- 3/4 cup all-purpose flour

Instructions:

1. Set your oven to 350°F (180°C) and lightly grease a 9x9 inch baking pan.
2. In a mixing bowl, combine the sourdough discard, cocoa powder, sugar, melted butter, eggs, vanilla extract, and salt.
3. Gradually fold in the flour until just incorporated.
4. Transfer the batter to the prepared pan and bake for 20-25 minutes..
5. Allow to cool before cutting into squares.

Sourdough Discard Fritters

Ingredients:

- 1 cup sourdough discard
- 1 cup grated zucchini
- 1/4 cup grated Parmesan cheese
- 1 egg
- 1/2 cup all-purpose flour
- 1 teaspoon salt
- 1/2 teaspoon pepper
- 2 tablespoons olive oil for frying

Instructions:

1. In a bowl, combine the sourdough discard, zucchini, Parmesan cheese, and egg.
2. In a separate bowl, mix the flour, salt, and pepper.
3. Slowly incorporate the dry ingredients into the wet mixture, stirring until thoroughly combined.
4. Heat olive oil in a pan over medium-high heat.
5. Using a spoon or scoop, drop small amounts of batter into the hot oil.
6. Cook for 3-4 minutes on each side until golden brown.
7. Remove from heat and let cool before serving with your favorite dipping sauce.

Sourdough Discard Pretzels

Ingredients:

- 1 cup sourdough discard
- 1 cup warm water
- 2 1/2 cups all-purpose flour
- 1 tablespoon sugar
- 2 teaspoons salt
- 1 pack (7g) instant yeast
- 1/4 cup baking soda
- Coarse salt for topping

Instructions:

1. In a large bowl, mix together the sourdough discard and warm water.
2. Add in the flour, sugar, salt, and yeast. Mix until a dough forms.
3. Knead the dough on a floured surface for 5 minutes.
4. Place the dough in an oiled bowl, cover with plastic wrap, and let it rise for 1 hour.
5. Set the oven to 450°F (230°C) and cover a baking tray with parchment paper.
6. Divide the dough into small pieces and roll each piece into a rope shape.
7. Twist each rope into a pretzel shape and place on the prepared baking sheet.

8. In another bowl, combine the baking soda with 4 cups of hot water.
9. Dip each pretzel into the baking soda mixture for a few seconds, then place back on the baking sheet.
10. Sprinkle coarse salt over the top of each pretzel.
11. Bake for 12-15 minutes or until golden brown.
12. Let cool before serving with your favorite dipping sauce!

Sourdough Discard Dumplings

Ingredients:

- 1 cup sourdough discard
- 1 cup all-purpose flour
- 1/2 teaspoon baking powder
- 1/2 teaspoon salt
- 1/4 cup milk
- 2 tablespoons butter

Instructions:

- In a mixing bowl, combine the sourdough discard, flour, baking powder, and salt.
- In a saucepan, gently heat the milk and butter until the butter is fully melted.
- Pour the warm milk mixture into the dry ingredients and stir until a dough forms.
- Drop spoonfuls of the dough into simmering soup or stew and cook for 10 minutes.
- Serve alongside your favorite dish or enjoy as a cozy snack.

Sourdough Discard Bagels

Ingredients:

- 1 cup sourdough discard
- 1 cup warm water
- 3 cups bread flour
- 1 tablespoon sugar
- 2 teaspoons salt
- 1 pack (7g) instant yeast
- 1/4 cup baking soda
- Toppings (sesame seeds, poppy seeds, etc.)

Instructions:

1. In a mixing bowl, combine the sourdough discard, warm water, flour, sugar, salt, and yeast. Stir until a cohesive dough forms.
2. Knead the dough for 5 minutes, then allow it to rise for 1 hour.
3. Divide the dough into equal portions and shape each portion into bagels.
4. Boil a pot of water and add baking soda. Cook the bagels for 30 seconds on each side.
5. Move the boiled bagels to a parchment-lined baking sheet and add your favorite toppings.
6. Bake in a preheated oven at 425°F (218°C) for 25-30 minutes, or until they are golden brown.

Sourdough Discard Cornbread

Ingredients:

- 1 cup sourdough discard
- 1 cup cornmeal
- 1 cup all-purpose flour
- 1/4 cup sugar
- 1 tablespoon baking powder
- 1/2 teaspoon salt
- 1/2 cup melted butter
- 1 cup milk
- 2 eggs

Instructions:

1. In a mixing bowl, combine the sourdough discard, cornmeal, flour, sugar, baking powder, and salt.
2. In another bowl, beat the eggs, then mix in the melted butter and milk.
3. Gently fold the wet ingredients into the dry mixture until just combined.
4. Transfer the batter to a greased 9x9-inch baking dish.
5. Bake in a preheated oven at 375°F (190°C) for 25-30 minutes, or until the top is golden brown.

Sourdough Discard Cheese Crackers

Ingredients:

- 1 cup sourdough discard
- 1 cup shredded cheddar cheese
- 1 cup all-purpose flour
- 1/4 cup butter, softened
- 1/2 teaspoon salt
- 1/2 teaspoon paprika

Instructions:

1. Heat your oven to 350°F (180°C) and cover a baking tray with parchment paper.
2. In a mixer, blend all the ingredients until a smooth dough forms.
3. Roll out the dough on a floured surface and cut it into your preferred shapes.
4. Arrange the crackers on the prepared baking sheet and bake for 15-20 minutes, or until they are golden brown and crispy.

Sourdough Discard Lemon Bars

Ingredients:

- 1 cup sourdough discard
- 1 cup all-purpose flour
- 1/2 cup butter, softened
- 1/4 cup powdered sugar
- 4 eggs
- 1 1/2 cups sugar
- 1/4 cup lemon juice
- 1 teaspoon of grated lemon peel

Instructions:

1. Heat the oven to 350°F (175°C) and cover a baking tray with parchment paper.
2. In a bowl, mix the sourdough discard, flour, butter, and powdered sugar until it forms a dough.
3. Press into the prepared dish and bake for 20 minutes.
4. In a separate bowl, combine the eggs, sugar, lemon juice, and zest using a whisk.
5. Pour the mixture onto the baked crust and place it back in the oven for another 20 minutes.
6. Let cool before slicing into bars.

Sourdough Discard Garlic Knots

Ingredients:

- 1 cup sourdough discard
- 1 cup warm water
- 2 1/2 cups all-purpose flour
- 1 tablespoon sugar
- 1 teaspoon salt
- 1 pack (7g) instant yeast
- 1/4 cup melted butter
- 1 tablespoon minced garlic
- 1 teaspoon parsley

Instructions:

1. In a large bowl, mix the sourdough discard, water, flour, sugar, salt, and yeast until it forms a dough.
2. Knead the dough for 5-7 minutes on a floured surface.
3. Place in a greased bowl and let it rise for an hour.
4. Punch down the dough and roll into long ropes.
5. Tie each rope into a knot and place on a baking sheet lined with parchment paper.
6. Bake at 375°F (190°C) for 20 minutes until golden brown.
7. Mix melted butter, garlic, and parsley in a small bowl and brush over the hot knots before serving.

Sourdough Discard Pancake Bites

Ingredients:

- 1 cup sourdough discard
- 1 cup all-purpose flour
- 1/2 cup milk
- 1 egg
- 1 tablespoon sugar
- 1 teaspoon baking powder
- 1/2 teaspoon salt
- 1/2 teaspoon vanilla extract
- 2 tablespoons melted butter

Instructions:

1. In a mixing bowl, combine the sourdough discard, flour, milk, egg, sugar, baking powder, salt, and vanilla extract.
2. Mix thoroughly and allow the batter to rest for 10-15 minutes to thicken.
3. Warm up a non-stick skillet on medium heat and gently coat it with melted butter.
4. Using a spoon or small cookie scoop, drop spoonfuls of batter onto the pan.
5. Cook for 1-2 minutes on each side until they turn golden brown.
6. Serve warm with maple syrup or your favorite toppings.

Sourdough Discard Oatmeal Cookies

Ingredients:

- 1 cup sourdough discard
- 1 cup rolled oats
- 3/4 cup all-purpose flour
- 1/2 cup butter, softened
- 1/2 cup brown sugar
- 1/4 cup sugar
- 1 egg
- 1 teaspoon vanilla extract
- 1/2 teaspoon baking soda
- 1/2 teaspoon cinnamon
- 1/4 teaspoon salt

Instructions:

1. Set your oven to 350°F (175°C) and cover a baking tray with parchment paper.
2. In a mixing bowl, cream the butter, brown sugar, and granulated sugar together until the mixture is light and fluffy.
3. Beat in the egg, vanilla extract, and sourdough discard until well combined.
4. In another bowl, whisk the oats, flour, baking soda, cinnamon, and salt together.
5. Gradually incorporate the dry ingredients into the wet mixture, stirring until just combined.

6. Drop spoonfuls of dough onto the prepared baking sheet and bake for 10-12 minutes, or until golden.

Sourdough Discard Cheese Biscuits

Ingredients:

- 2 cups of all-purpose flour
- 1 cup of sourdough discard
- 1 cup of grated cheddar cheese
- 1/2 teaspoon of salt
- 1 tablespoon of baking powder
- 1/2 cup of cubed cold butter
- 1/2 cup of milk

Instructions:

1. Heat your oven to 425°F (220°C) and line a baking sheet with parchment paper.
2. In a large bowl, combine flour, cheese, baking powder, and salt.
3. Incorporate cold butter cubes using your fingers or a pastry cutter, mixing until the mixture resembles coarse crumbs.
4. Carefully mix in the sourdough discard and milk, folding until just incorporated.
5. Place spoonfuls of the dough onto the prepared baking sheet and bake for 15-20 minutes until they turn golden brown.
6. Enjoy warm as a delightful side dish or snack.

Sourdough Discard Chocolate Muffins

Ingredients:

1. 1 cup sourdough discard
2. 1 1/2 cups all-purpose flour
3. 1/2 cup cocoa powder
4. 1/2 cup sugar
5. 1/2 cup milk
6. 1/4 cup vegetable oil
7. 1 egg
8. 1 teaspoon baking powder
9. 1/2 teaspoon salt
10. 1/2 cup chocolate chips

Instructions:

1. Set your oven to 375°F (190°C) and prepare a muffin tin by placing paper liners in each cup.
2. In a mixing bowl, blend the flour, cocoa powder, sugar, baking powder, and salt together.
3. In another bowl, whisk the sourdough discard, milk, vegetable oil, and egg together.
4. Gradually incorporate the wet ingredients into the dry mixture, gently stirring until just combined.
5. Carefully incorporate the chocolate chips by folding them into the mixture.
6. Fill each muffin tin to about three-quarters of its capacity with the batter.

7. Bake for 18 to 20 minutes, checking doneness by inserting a toothpick into the center; it should come out clean.

Sourdough Discard Tortillas

Ingredients:

- 1 cup sourdough discard
- 2 cups all-purpose flour
- 1/3 cup vegetable oil
- 1 teaspoon salt
- 3/4 cup warm water

Instructions:

1. In a mixing bowl, combine the sourdough discard, flour, vegetable oil, and salt.
2. Gradually incorporate warm water until a cohesive dough forms.
3. Knead the dough on a floured surface for 5 minutes.
4. Divide the dough into 8 equal portions and roll each into thin rounds.
5. Heat a skillet over medium-high heat and cook each tortilla for approximately 2 minutes on each side.
6. Serve with your favorite fillings or use them as a base for homemade pizzas.

Sourdough Discard Apple Cake

Ingredients:

- 1 cup sourdough discard
- 1 1/2 cups all-purpose flour
- 1 cup sugar
- 1/2 cup vegetable oil
- 2 eggs
- 1 teaspoon baking powder
- 1/2 teaspoon cinnamon
- 1/4 teaspoon nutmeg
- 1/4 teaspoon salt
- 2 cups diced apples

Instructions:

1. Set your oven to 350°F (175°C). As it heats, lightly grease a 9x13 inch baking dish with butter or cooking spray for easy removal later.
2. In a large mixing bowl, combine the sourdough discard, flour, sugar, vegetable oil, and eggs. Use a whisk or electric mixer to blend until smooth, creating a thick batter.
3. Once smooth, add the baking powder, ground cinnamon, nutmeg, and a pinch of salt. Stir until fully incorporated to ensure even flavor distribution.

4. Gently fold in the diced apples for texture and sweetness. Mix carefully to avoid breaking them up too much.
5. Transfer the batter into the greased baking dish and evenly distribute it using a spatula.Cook in the preheated oven for 35-40 minutes.Test for doneness by inserting a toothpick into the center; it should emerge clean.
6. After baking, remove from the oven and let it cool slightly. Serve warm, and consider topping with powdered sugar or whipped cream for an extra treat.

Sourdough Discard Pita Bread

Ingredients:

- 1 cup sourdough discard
- 2 cups all-purpose flour
- 1/2 cup warm water
- 1 tablespoon olive oil
- 1 teaspoon salt
- 1 teaspoon sugar
- 1 teaspoon instant yeast

Instructions:

1. In a large mixing bowl, combine sourdough discard, warm water, and sugar, stirring until the mixture is well blended and the sugar is completely dissolved.
2. Gradually stir in salt and instant yeast, ensuring the yeast is evenly distributed throughout the mixture. Then, slowly incorporate flour, adding it in increments until a cohesive dough starts to form, ensuring that all dry ingredients are well integrated.
3. When the mixture forms, knead it on a lightly floured surface for approximately 5 minutes. Keep kneading until the dough is smooth, elastic, and slightly sticky, signaling that the gluten has developed correctly.
4. Transfer the kneaded dough to a lightly oiled bowl, turning the dough to coat it in oil. Cover the bowl with a clean towel or plastic wrap, and allow it to rise in a

warm, draft-free area for about 1 hour, or until the dough has doubled in size.

5. After the dough has risen, gently punch it down to release any trapped air bubbles. Separate the dough into even pieces, forming each into a ball roughly the size of a golf ball.
6. On a generously floured surface, take each dough ball and roll it out with a rolling pin into a thin, even circle, aiming for a thickness of about 1/4 inch to achieve a perfect pita bread texture.
7. Preheat a skillet or griddle over medium-high heat, allowing it to reach the right temperature. Once hot, carefully place each rolled-out pita onto the skillet and cook for 2-3 minutes on each side. You'll know they are ready when they puff up and turn lightly browned with a slight char.
8. Serve the warm pitas immediately, accompanied by your favorite fillings, spreads, or dips like hummus, tzatziki, or grilled vegetables, making for a delicious and versatile meal.

Sourdough Discard Peanut Butter Cookies

Ingredients:

- 1 cup sourdough discard
- 1 cup all-purpose flour
- 1/2 cup peanut butter
- 1/2 cup butter, softened
- 1/2 cup sugar
- 1/2 cup brown sugar
- 1 egg
- 1/2 teaspoon baking soda
- 1/4 teaspoon salt

Instructions:

1. Preheat your oven to 350°F (175°C) and cover a lined baking tray with parchment paper, ensuring it's evenly coated to stop sticking and simplify cleanup.
2. In a big mixing bowl, combine the softened butter, smooth peanut butter, white sugar, and brown sugar. Use an electric mixer or a wooden spoon to combine them until the mixture becomes smooth, light, and fluffy, taking approximately 2-3 minutes.
3. Once the mixture is fluffy, carefully incorporate the egg and sourdough discard, mixing until everything is well combined and the batter is smooth.
4. In another bowl, whisk the all-purpose flour, baking soda, and salt until they are well blended. This step is

crucial for ensuring that the leavening agent is distributed throughout the flour.

5. Slowly incorporate the dry ingredients into the wet mixture, gently stirring until just blended. Be careful not to overmix, as this can affect the texture of your cookies.

6. With a spoon or cookie scoop, place generous portions of the dough onto the lined baking sheet, ensuring they are spaced a few inches apart to accommodate spreading while baking. Place in your preheated oven for 10-12 minutes, until the edges of the cookies turn golden brown and the centers appear slightly soft.

Sourdough Discard Blueberry Muffins

Ingredients:

- 1 cup of leftover sourdough starter
- 1 and 1/2 cups of plain flour
- 1/2 cup of granulated sugar
- 1/2 cup of milk
- 1/4 cup of vegetable oil
- 1 egg
- 1 teaspoon of baking powder
- 1/2 teaspoon of salt
- 1 cup fresh blueberries

Instructions:

1. Set your oven to 375°F (190°C) and prepare a muffin tin by placing paper liners in each cup.
2. In a mixing bowl, combine the sourdough discard, milk, oil, and egg until well blended.
3. In another bowl, whisk the flour, sugar, baking powder, and salt together.
4. Gradually incorporate the dry ingredients into the wet mixture, stirring until just combined.
5. Carefully incorporate the blueberries, ensuring you do not overmix.
6. Distribute the batter evenly in the muffin tins and cook for 18 to 20 minutes, or until they achieve a golden brown color.

Sourdough Discard Savory Pancakes

Ingredients:

- 1 cup sourdough discard
- 1 cup all-purpose flour
- 1 cup milk
- 1 egg
- 1 tablespoon olive oil
- 1 teaspoon baking powder
- 1/2 teaspoon salt
- 1/2 cup chopped spinach
- 1/4 cup feta cheese, crumbled

Instructions:

1. In a large mixing bowl, combine the sourdough discard, flour, milk, egg, and olive oil until the mixture is smooth and well blended, ensuring there are no lumps. This combination creates a flavorful base for your pancakes.
2. Next, add the baking powder and salt, stirring gently to incorporate them into the batter without overmixing, as this will help achieve a light and fluffy texture.
3. Carefully fold in the chopped spinach and crumbled feta cheese, making sure they are evenly distributed throughout the batter for a burst of flavor in every bite.
4. Warm a non-stick skillet on medium heat, lightly greasing it with cooking spray or a pat of butter to

prevent the pancakes from sticking and to add a touch of richness.

5. For each pancake, pour 1/4 cup of the batter onto the pan, leaving enough space between each one to allow for spreading as they cook.
6. Cook the pancakes for 2-3 minutes on one side until bubbles begin to appear on the surface, signaling that they're ready to be flipped. Gently flip the pancakes and cook for an additional 1-2 minutes on the other side until golden brown and cooked through.
7. Serve the pancakes warm, topped with your favorite additions, such as creamy avocado slices, a drizzle of honey for sweetness, or even a dollop of yogurt for extra flavor and texture.

Sourdough Discard Chocolate Chip Scones

Ingredients:

- 1 cup sourdough discard
- 2 cups all-purpose flour
- 1/4 cup sugar
- 1 tablespoon baking powder
- 1/2 teaspoon salt
- 1/2 cup cold unsalted butter, cubed
- 1/2 cup mini chocolate chips
- 1/2 cup heavy cream

Instructions:

1. Heat your oven to 400°F (200°C) and line a baking sheet with parchment paper.
2. In a large mixing bowl, combine the sourdough discard, flour, sugar, baking powder, and salt.
3. Using a pastry cutter or your fingers, cut in the cold butter until the mixture resembles coarse crumbs.
4. Gently fold in the mini chocolate chips.
5. Gradually pour in the heavy cream while stirring until just combined.
6. Turn out the dough onto a floured surface and shape it into a 1-inch thick circle.
7. Cut the circle into 8 equal wedges and place them on the prepared baking sheet.

8. Bake for 15-18 minutes, or until the scones are golden brown on top.
9. Let them cool for a few minutes before serving with a dollop of whipped cream and some extra chocolate chips on top.

Sourdough Discard Garlic Herb Breadsticks

Ingredients:

- 1 cup sourdough discard
- 2 cups all-purpose flour
- 1/2 cup warm water
- 1 tablespoon olive oil
- 1 teaspoon salt
- 1 teaspoon sugar
- 1 teaspoon instant yeast
- 1 tablespoon minced garlic
- 1 teaspoon dried herbs (oregano, basil, or thyme)

Instructions:

1. In a large mixing bowl, combine sourdough discard, flour, warm water, olive oil, salt, sugar, and yeast.
2. Knead the dough for 5-10 minutes until smooth and elastic.
3. Cover the bowl with plastic wrap and let it rise for 1 hour in a warm place.
4. Preheat the oven to 375°F (190°C) and line a baking sheet with parchment paper.
5. On a floured surface, roll out the dough into a rectangle about 1/2 inch thick.
6. Sprinkle minced garlic and dried herbs evenly over the dough.

7. Cut strips of dough about 1 inch wide and twist them into breadsticks.
8. Place the breadsticks on the prepared baking sheet and bake for 20-25 minutes until golden brown.
9. Serve warm with your favorite dipping sauce or enjoy them on their own.

Sourdough Discard Apple Fritters

Ingredients:

- 1 cup sourdough discard
- 1 cup all-purpose flour
- 1/4 cup sugar
- 1 teaspoon baking powder
- 1/2 teaspoon cinnamon
- 1/4 teaspoon salt
- 1/2 cup milk
- 1 egg
- 1 cup chopped apples
- Oil for frying

Instructions:

1. In a mixing bowl, combine flour, sugar, baking powder, cinnamon, and salt.
2. In another bowl, whisk together the sourdough discard, milk, and egg until smooth.
3. Gradually incorporate the wet mixture into the dry ingredients, stirring until fully combined.
4. Gently fold in the chopped apples.
5. Heat oil in a deep pan or fryer to 375°F (190°C).
6. Using a small scoop or spoon, drop the batter into the hot oil and fry for 2-3 minutes on each side, or until golden brown.

7. Remove from the oil and drain on paper towels, then sprinkle with powdered sugar before serving.

Sourdough Discard Pizza Rolls

Ingredients:

- 1 cup sourdough discard
- 2 cups all-purpose flour
- 1/2 cup warm water
- 1 tablespoon olive oil
- 1 teaspoon salt
- 1 teaspoon sugar
- 1 teaspoon instant yeast
- 1/2 cup pizza sauce
- 1 cup shredded mozzarella cheese
- Pepperoni slices (optional)

Instructions:

1. Mix warm water, sugar, and yeast in a bowl and let sit for 5 minutes.
2. Add sourdough discard, olive oil, salt, and flour, mixing into a dough.
3. Knead for 5 minutes, then let rise for 1 hour.
4. Preheat the oven to 375°F (190°C).
5. Roll out the dough into a rectangle on a floured surface.
6. Spread pizza sauce over the dough and sprinkle with cheese.
7. Add pepperoni slices if desired.
8. Roll up tightly and cut into slices.

9. Place slices on a baking sheet lined with parchment paper.
10. Bake for 20-25 minutes, until golden and cheese is melted.

Sourdough Discard Carrot Cake

Ingredients:

- 1 cup sourdough discard
- 1 1/2 cups all-purpose flour
- 1 cup sugar
- 1/2 cup vegetable oil
- 2 eggs
- 1 teaspoon baking powder
- 1/2 teaspoon cinnamon
- 1/4 teaspoon nutmeg
- 1/4 teaspoon salt
- 1 cup grated carrots

Instructions:

1. Set your oven to 350°F (180°C) and lightly grease a 9-inch cake pan with butter or cooking spray to ensure easy cake release after baking.
2. In a mixing bowl, combine the all-purpose flour, granulated sugar, baking powder, ground cinnamon, nutmeg, and salt, stirring thoroughly to evenly distribute the dry ingredients and enhance the flavor profile of your cake.
3. In another bowl, whisk the sourdough discard, which adds a unique tanginess and moisture, with the vegetable oil for richness, and the eggs to bind the ingredients together.

4. Gradually blend the wet ingredients into the dry mixture, stirring gently until just combined to avoid overmixing. Next, gently fold in the freshly grated carrots, which not only provide natural sweetness but also add a delightful texture to the batter.
5. Transfer the batter into the prepared cake pan, using a spatula to evenly spread it for a consistent rise during baking.
6. Bake in the preheated oven for 35-40 minutes, or until a toothpick inserted into the center comes out clean, indicating that the cake is fully cooked. Keep an eye on it towards the end of the baking time to prevent overbaking.
7. Once baked, allow the cake to cool in the pan for about 10 minutes before transferring it to a wire rack to cool completely. Before serving, consider topping it with a creamy cream cheese frosting for an extra touch of indulgence that perfectly complements the flavors of the cake.

Sourdough Discard Soft Pretzels

Ingredients:

- 1 cup sourdough discard
- 1 cup warm water
- 2 1/2 cups all-purpose flour
- 1 tablespoon sugar
- 2 teaspoons salt
- 1 pack (7g) instant yeast
- 1/4 cup baking soda
- Coarse salt for topping

Instructions:

1. Begin by preheating your oven to 450°F (230°C) to ensure it's hot enough for a perfect bake. While the oven heats up, line a baking sheet with parchment paper to prevent sticking and make for easy cleanup later.
2. In a mixing bowl, combine about 1 cup of warm water with 1 tablespoon of sugar and 2 tablespoons of active dry yeast. Mix gently and allow the mixture to sit for approximately 5 minutes until it becomes frothy, indicating that the yeast is activated and ready to work its magic.
3. Once the yeast mixture is bubbly, incorporate 1 cup of sourdough discard, 4 cups of all-purpose flour, and 1 teaspoon of salt. Stir the ingredients together until a

dough begins to form. Turn the mixture out onto a floured surface and knead for about 5 minutes, ensuring the dough is smooth and elastic.

4. Put the kneaded dough into a bowl with a light coating of oil, drape a damp cloth over it and let it rise for 30 minutes in a warm area. This resting period allows the dough to double in size, which is essential for achieving a light texture. After rising, divide the dough into equal portions and shape each piece into classic pretzel forms.

5. In a large pot, bring about 10 cups of water to a boil. Once boiling, carefully add 2/3 cup of baking soda to the pot. This step is crucial as it gives the pretzels their distinctive golden-brown color and chewy exterior. Gently lower each shaped pretzel into the boiling water, allowing them to boil for about 30 seconds each. Use a slotted spoon to remove them and drain any excess water.

6. Transfer the boiled pretzels to the prepared baking sheet, ensuring they are spaced apart. Generously sprinkle coarse salt over the top of each pretzel for that classic flavor. Finally, put the baking sheet into the preheated oven and bake for 12-14 minutes, or until the pretzels become golden brown and emit a delightful aroma.

Sourdough Discard Snickerdoodles

Ingredients:

- 1 cup of sourdough starter discard
- 1 and 1/2 cups of all-purpose flour
- 1/2 cup of softened butter
- 1 cup of granulated sugar
- 1 egg
- 1 teaspoon of vanilla extract
- 1/2 teaspoon of baking soda
- 1/2 teaspoon of cream of tartar
- 1/4 teaspoon of salt
- 2 tablespoons of sugar
- 2 teaspoons of cinnamon

Instructions:

1. Set your oven to 350°F (175°C) and cover a baking sheet with parchment paper.
2. In a mixing bowl, cream together the butter and sugar until the mixture is light and fluffy, then incorporate the egg and vanilla extract.
3. Gently fold in the sourdough discard.
4. In a different bowl, combine the flour, baking soda, cream of tartar, and salt, mixing them thoroughly.
5. Slowly mix the dry ingredients into the wet mixture, stirring until just blended.

6. In a small bowl, mix 2 tablespoons of sugar with cinnamon. Shape the dough into balls and roll them in the cinnamon-sugar mix before arranging them on the prepared baking sheet.
7. Bake for 10-12 minutes, or until the edges are set.

Sourdough Discard Veggie Frittata

Ingredients:

- 1 cup sourdough discard
- 6 eggs
- 1/2 cup milk
- 1 cup chopped vegetables (bell peppers, onions, spinach)
- 1/2 cup shredded cheese
- Salt and pepper to taste

Instructions:

1. Begin by preheating your oven to 375°F (190°C), ensuring it's at the right temperature for even baking.
2. In a large mixing bowl, combine the sourdough discard, eggs, and milk, whisking them together until the mixture is smooth and well blended.
3. Gently fold in your choice of chopped vegetables, such as bell peppers, spinach, or onions, along with a generous amount of shredded cheese, like cheddar or mozzarella, to add flavor and richness.
4. Don't forget to season your mixture with salt and pepper to taste, enhancing the overall flavor profile.
5. Carefully pour the combined mixture into a greased 9-inch pie dish, spreading it evenly to ensure uniform cooking.

6. Put the dish in the oven and let it bake for 25-30 minutes, or until the mixture is set in the center and has developed a beautiful golden brown top, signaling that it's ready.
7. Once baked, remove the dish from the oven and let it cool slightly before serving it hot or at room temperature, perfect for any meal or gathering.

Sourdough Discard Banana Oat Muffins

Ingredients:

- 1 cup sourdough discard
- 1 cup mashed bananas
- 1 cup rolled oats
- 1/2 cup all-purpose flour
- 1/4 cup sugar
- 1/2 cup milk
- 1/4 cup vegetable oil
- 1 egg
- 1 teaspoon baking powder
- 1/2 teaspoon cinnamon
- 1/4 teaspoon salt

Instructions:

1. Set your oven to 375°F (190°C) and insert paper liners into a muffin tin to simplify muffin removal once baked.
2. In a large mixing bowl, mix the mashed bananas with sourdough discard, milk, vegetable oil, and a beaten egg, stirring until the mixture is smooth and well blended.
3. In another bowl, whisk the dry ingredients: rolled oats, all-purpose flour, granulated sugar, baking powder, ground cinnamon, and a pinch of salt, ensuring they are evenly distributed.

4. Gently incorporate the dry mixture into the wet ingredients, stirring slowly until they are just blended. Be careful not to overmix, as this can lead to dense muffins.
5. Evenly distribute the batter into the lined muffin cups, filling each one approximately two-thirds full. Place in the preheated oven and bake for 18-20 minutes, checking doneness by inserting a toothpick into the center of a muffin; it should come out clean.

Sourdough Discard Jalapeño Cornbread

Ingredients:

- 1 cup sourdough discard
- 1 cup cornmeal
- 1 cup all-purpose flour
- 1/4 cup sugar
- 1 tablespoon baking powder
- 1/2 teaspoon salt
- 1/2 cup melted butter
- 1 cup milk
- 2 eggs
- 1/2 cup chopped jalapeños

Instructions:

1. Begin by preheating your oven to 400°F (200°C) and lightly greasing a baking dish with butter or cooking spray to ensure your dish doesn't stick.
2. In a mixing bowl, blend the cornmeal, flour, sugar, baking powder, and salt, whisking until the mixture is smooth and lump-free.
3. In another bowl, whisk the melted butter—after letting it cool slightly—along with the milk, eggs, and sourdough discard until the mixture is smooth and consistent.
4. Gently fold the dry ingredients into the wet mixture using a spatula, being careful not to overmix; you want

to combine them just until all the flour is moistened and no dry spots remain.
5. Stir in the diced jalapeños for a spicy kick, evenly spread the batter into the baking dish that has been prepared.
6. Place in the preheated oven and bake for 25-30 minutes, or until the surface is golden brown and a toothpick inserted into the center emerges clean.

Sourdough Discard Rosemary Focaccia

Ingredients:

- 1 cup sourdough discard
- 2 cups all-purpose flour
- 1/2 cup warm water
- 1/4 cup olive oil
- 1 teaspoon salt

Instructions:

1. In a bowl, mix warm water, 2 tablespoons olive oil, and sourdough discard until combined.
2. Add flour and salt, mixing to form a dough. Knead for about 5 minutes until smooth.
3. Place the dough in an oiled bowl, cover, and let rise for 1 hour.
4. Preheat the oven to 400°F (200°C).
5. Press the dough into a greased baking pan, drizzle with remaining olive oil, and sprinkle with rosemary.
6. Use your fingers to dimple the surface and let it rest for 15 minutes.
7. Bake for 20-25 minutes until golden brown.

7-Step Plan to Get Started with Sourdough Discard

Now that you have some tasty recipes to use up your sourdough discard, it's time to learn how to incorporate this valuable ingredient into your baking routine. Here is a 7-step plan on how to get started with sourdough discard.

Step 1: Gather Ingredients and Tools

When beginning your journey with sourdough discard baking, it's crucial to assemble the right ingredients and tools to set yourself up for success. Here's a detailed guide to help you understand the role of each ingredient and the importance of having the right tools at your disposal.

Ingredients:

- ***All-Purpose Flour***: This is the backbone of most baking recipes, providing structure and stability. Its protein content creates gluten, which helps dough rise and maintain its shape. For those with dietary restrictions, alternatives like whole wheat or

gluten-free flours can be used, though they might alter the texture.
- *Sugar*: Beyond adding sweetness, sugar plays a vital role in browning and moisture retention. It helps create a tender crumb and can also aid in leavening when creamed with butter.
- *Eggs*: Eggs are multifunctional in baking; they add moisture, bind ingredients, contribute to the structure, and can introduce richness and color. If you're vegan or allergic, consider substitutes like flaxseed meal mixed with water or commercial egg replacers.
- *Milk*: Adding moisture and richness, milk enhances the texture and flavor of your baked goods. It can be replaced with non-dairy alternatives like almond or soy milk for those with lactose intolerance.
- *Butter*: Butter adds flavor and a tender texture to baked goods. It can be substituted with margarine or shortening if necessary.
- *Baking Powder*: This leavening agent helps your baked goods rise by releasing carbon dioxide when exposed to moisture and heat. Ensure it's fresh for the best results since its effectiveness decreases over time.
- *Sourdough Discard*: The star ingredient, sourdough discard, adds a unique tangy flavor and can enhance the texture of your baked goods. It's a great way to reduce waste while adding depth to your recipes.

Tools:

- ***Measuring Cups and Spoons***: Precision is key in baking, and these tools ensure you add the right amount of each ingredient. For dry ingredients, use the scoop and sweep method; for liquid ingredients, use a clear measuring cup to eye the correct amount.
- ***Mixing Bowl***: A sturdy mixing bowl is essential for combining your ingredients. Opt for a set that includes various sizes to accommodate different recipe needs.
- ***Whisk or Spoon***: These tools are vital for mixing wet and dry ingredients. A whisk is particularly useful for incorporating air, which can help achieve a lighter texture.
- ***Baking Sheet***: Ideal for cookies, scones, and other baked goods, a baking sheet ensures even baking. Line it with parchment paper to prevent sticking and make cleanup easier.
- ***Oven***: Your primary baking appliance, the oven should be preheated to the correct temperature as specified in your recipe. An oven thermometer can be helpful to ensure accuracy.

Organizing Your Kitchen Space:

Create a dedicated baking area to streamline your process. Keep your ingredients and tools within arm's reach, and consider setting up a clean counter space for mixing and assembling. Label storage containers for quick ingredient identification and maintain a tidy workspace to enhance efficiency.

Tips and Alternatives:

If you lack a specific tool, improvise with what you have. For example, a fork can substitute for a whisk, or a glass can stand in for a rolling pin. Similarly, if you're missing an ingredient, research potential substitutes online, keeping in mind that they may alter the final product's texture or flavor.

By understanding the role of each ingredient and using the right tools, you'll find the baking process much smoother and more enjoyable.

Step 2: Understand Sourdough Discard

Sourdough discard is an integral part of the sourdough baking process, especially for beginners looking to explore its potential in various recipes. Here's a comprehensive guide to understanding and utilizing sourdough discard effectively:

What is Sourdough Discard?

Sourdough discard is the portion of sourdough starter that is removed during the feeding process. Unlike the active starter, which is bubbly and ready for bread-making after being fed with fresh flour and water, the discard is often unfed and less active. However, it still contains wild yeast and bacteria, offering a unique tangy flavor that can enhance many baked goods.

Difference Between Discard and Active Starter:

- Discard: Generally kept in the fridge, discard is not as bubbly but still has a mild fermentation flavor. It's perfect for recipes that do not rely on strong leavening action.
- Active Starter: Fed regularly, it's bubbly and strong enough to leaven bread. It is used when an airy, risen dough is desired.

Benefits of Using Sourdough Discard:

1. *Flavor Enhancement*: The tangy, slightly sour taste of discard adds complexity to recipes, making them more interesting and flavorful.
2. *Waste Reduction*: Regularly discarding part of your starter to keep it healthy can feel wasteful. Using the discard in recipes helps reduce this waste.
3. *Versatility*: Discard can be used in a variety of recipes, from pancakes and waffles to cakes and crackers.

Proper Storage of Sourdough Discard:

- *Refrigeration*: Store sourdough discard in a sealed container in the fridge. This slows down fermentation and keeps it usable for longer.
- *Shelf Life*: Generally, sourdough discard can be kept in the fridge for up to a week. However, it's best to use it sooner to maintain optimal flavor and prevent spoilage.

- ***Signs of Spoilage***: If the discard develops an off smell, mold, or an unusual color, it's best to discard it and start fresh.

Incorporating Sourdough Discard into Recipes:
- ***Adjusting Recipes***: Since sourdough discard has a liquid consistency, recipes using it may require adjustments in liquid and flour ratios. Typically, the discard can replace an equivalent amount of liquid and a small amount of flour in a recipe.
- ***Mix and Match***: Start by incorporating discard into recipes that naturally accommodate extra liquid, like pancakes or muffins. Gradually experiment by substituting part of the flour and liquid in other recipes.
- ***Stir Before Using***: Before adding discard to a recipe, give it a good stir to ensure even distribution of its natural yeast and bacterial cultures.

By understanding and utilizing sourdough discard effectively, you can enhance your baking repertoire, reduce waste, and enjoy the delightful flavors it brings to your creations.

Step 3: Start with Simple Recipes

Embarking on your sourdough discard baking journey can be exciting, and beginning with simple recipes is a great way to ease into the process while building your confidence. Here's why starting with easy recipes like pancakes or muffins is beneficial and how you can make the most of this step.

Why Start with Simple Recipes?

1. *Forgiving Nature*: Recipes like pancakes or muffins are forgiving, meaning they can withstand minor errors in measurement or technique without drastically affecting the final product. This allows beginners to experiment and learn without the pressure of perfection.
2. *Quick Results*: These recipes often require minimal preparation time and have shorter baking times, providing instant gratification and keeping motivation high.
3. *Foundation Building*: Simple recipes help you grasp fundamental baking principles such as mixing, measuring, and understanding texture and consistency, which are crucial for more advanced baking endeavors.

Tips for Selecting Beginner-Friendly Recipes:

- *Minimal Ingredients*: Look for recipes that use basic pantry staples like flour, sugar, eggs, butter, and milk. This reduces complexity and helps you focus on mastering techniques rather than sourcing ingredients.
- *Clear Instructions*: Choose recipes with step-by-step instructions that are easy to follow. Visual guides or

video tutorials can also be helpful in understanding each stage of the process.
- *Familiarity*: Start with recipes you're familiar with or have enjoyed making in the past. This familiarity can boost your confidence and make the learning process more enjoyable.

Understanding Basic Baking Techniques:
- *Mixing*: Learn the difference between folding and stirring, and how to avoid overmixing, which can lead to tough baked goods.
- *Measuring*: Practice accurate measuring of both dry and wet ingredients to ensure consistent results.
- *Temperature Awareness*: Understand the importance of preheating the oven and how temperature affects baking times and outcomes.

Where to Find Beginner-Friendly Recipes:
- *Cookbooks and Websites*: Look for beginner-focused cookbooks or websites dedicated to sourdough baking. They often categorize recipes by difficulty, making it easier to find suitable options.
- *Online Communities*: Join baking forums or social media groups where you can share experiences and get recommendations for tried-and-tested beginner recipes.

Adapting Recipes for Sourdough Discard:

- ***Substitution Tips***: Replace part of the liquid and a small portion of the flour in your chosen recipe with sourdough discard. This not only reduces waste but also adds a unique flavor profile to your baked goods.
- ***Incremental Changes***: Start by adding a small amount of discard and gradually increase as you become more comfortable with its impact on texture and flavor.

Remember, baking is as much about the journey as it is about the final product. Don't be discouraged by mistakes; instead, use them as learning opportunities. Each baking session will enhance your skills, and soon you'll be ready to tackle more complex recipes. Stay curious, enjoy the process, and celebrate each success, no matter how small.

Step 4: Learn Basic Baking Techniques

Mastering basic baking techniques is essential for any beginner looking to improve their skills and achieve better outcomes in the kitchen. Understanding common baking terms and techniques like folding, creaming, and sifting can transform your baking experience, making it easier to follow recipes and experiment with new ones. Here's a closer look at these foundational skills:

Understanding Common Baking Terms and Techniques:

- *Folding*: This gentle mixing method is used to combine delicate ingredients, such as whipped cream or beaten egg whites, into a heavier mixture without deflating the air incorporated during whipping. It involves carefully lifting the mixture from the bottom of the bowl and folding it over the top, using a spatula. Folding is crucial in recipes like soufflés or mousse, where maintaining volume is essential.
- *Creaming*: Often used in cookie and cake recipes, creaming involves beating sugar and butter together until the mix is light and fluffy. This process incorporates air, which helps leaven the baked goods and creates a tender texture. Proper creaming can significantly affect the final product's lightness and rise.
- *Sifting*: Sifting involves passing flour or other dry ingredients through a sieve to remove lumps and aerate them. This ensures even mixing and helps prevent dense baked goods. Sifting is particularly important in recipes requiring precise ingredient distribution, like cakes and pastries.

Resources for Learning Baking Techniques:

- *Online Tutorials*: Websites like YouTube and baking blogs offer countless tutorial videos demonstrating various baking techniques. These visual guides can be

incredibly helpful in understanding the nuances of each method.
- ***Books and Guides***: Invest in beginner-friendly baking books that explain techniques with illustrations and step-by-step instructions. Many books also provide practice recipes to reinforce the skills learned.
- ***Baking Classes***: Consider enrolling in local or online baking classes that offer hands-on experience and personalized instruction. These classes can provide valuable feedback and boost your confidence.

Tips for Practicing Baking Techniques at Home:
- ***Start Small***: Practice techniques with simple recipes to focus solely on mastering the skill without getting overwhelmed by complex instructions.
- ***Repeat and Refine***: Regular practice is key. Repeat techniques multiple times to build muscle memory and refine your skills.
- ***Experiment***: Try different recipes that utilize the same technique to understand how it impacts different types of baked goods.
- ***Seek Feedback***: Share your baked goods with friends or family and seek their feedback to identify areas for improvement.

Benefits of Mastering Baking Techniques:

- *Improved Recipe Outcomes*: Understanding and applying the correct techniques can dramatically enhance the texture, flavor, and appearance of your baked goods.
- *Increased Confidence*: As you become more comfortable with these methods, your confidence in the kitchen will grow, encouraging you to tackle more challenging recipes.
- *Creative Freedom*: Mastery of basic techniques allows you to experiment and innovate, creating your own recipes or modifying existing ones to suit your taste.

By dedicating time to learn and practice these fundamental techniques, you'll lay a strong foundation for your baking journey. Each skill mastered brings you one step closer to becoming a more proficient and adventurous baker.

Step 5: Measure Accurately

In baking, precision is crucial. Unlike cooking, where adding a dash or a pinch can improve a dish, baking depends on exact measurements to achieve the desired results. Let's delve into why accurate measurements are essential and how you can master this crucial skill.

Why Accurate Measurements Matter:

1. ***Chemical Reactions***: Baking involves chemical reactions between ingredients, such as the activation of baking powder or yeast, which depend on precise quantities to work correctly. Too much or too little of an ingredient can alter the texture, rise, and flavor of your baked goods.
2. ***Consistency***: Consistent measurements ensure that your favorite recipes turn out the same every time. This reliability is essential when baking for special occasions or sharing recipes with others.
3. ***Texture and Flavor***: The right balance of ingredients affects the texture and flavor of your baked goods. Accurate measurements help achieve the desired crumb, moisture level, and taste.

Using Measuring Cups and Spoons:

- ***Dry Ingredients***: Use measuring cups for dry ingredients like flour, sugar, and cocoa powder. Scoop the ingredient into the cup, then use a straight edge, such as a knife, to level it off for an accurate measurement. Avoid packing ingredients like flour, which can lead to using too much.
- ***Wet Ingredients***: Use measuring spoons for small quantities of liquid and liquid measuring cups for larger amounts. Read the measurement at eye level to ensure accuracy, especially for liquids like milk or oil.

Common Measurement Mistakes to Avoid:

- *Scooping Flour*: Avoid scooping flour directly from the bag with your measuring cup, as it can pack the flour and lead to using more than intended. Instead, use a spoon to fill the cup and level it off.
- *Using Dry Cups for Liquids*: Dry measuring cups are not intended for liquids as they don't offer the same precision as liquid measuring cups, which have a spout for easy pouring.
- *Overfilling Spoons*: When measuring with spoons, ensure they're level and not heaping unless the recipe specifies otherwise.

Tools for Precision:

Kitchen Scales: Investing in a kitchen scale can significantly improve measurement accuracy, especially for ingredients like flour and sugar. Many recipes provide measurements in grams or ounces, offering a more precise approach than volume measurements.

Following Recipe Instructions:

- Read Thoroughly: Before you start, thoroughly read the recipe to understand the required measurements and techniques.

- Pre-Measure Ingredients: Gather and measure all ingredients before beginning to streamline the process and reduce the chance of errors.

Practicing Measurement Skills:
- *Practice Makes Perfect*: As with any skill, practice is key. Regular baking will help you become more familiar with measuring techniques and improve your accuracy over time.
- *Experiment with Scales*: If you're transitioning to using a kitchen scale, practice converting your favorite recipes from cups to grams or ounces to get comfortable with weight measurements.

By mastering the art of accurate measurements, you'll greatly enhance your baking prowess, resulting in delicious and consistent baked goods every time. Remember, precision is the foundation of baking success.

Step 6: Follow Recipes Carefully

In baking, following recipes carefully is a fundamental step that can significantly influence the success of your culinary creations. For beginners, understanding the intricacies of a recipe goes beyond just mixing ingredients—it's about appreciating the science and art involved in baking. Here's why this step is crucial and how you can master it.

Importance of Reading the Entire Recipe:

1. Understanding the Process: Before you even start gathering ingredients, read through the entire recipe to grasp the overall process. This helps you understand what to expect and prepares you for each step.
2. Timing and Preparation: Knowing the timing of each stage—whether it's preheating the oven, letting dough rise, or cooling baked goods—allows you to plan your activities efficiently. Some recipes might require ingredients to be at room temperature or dough to chill for a set period, so being aware of these details can prevent surprise delays.
3. Avoiding Mistakes: A full read-through helps you spot potential pitfalls, such as missing ingredients or unclear instructions, which you can address before starting.

Benefits of Following Steps Sequentially:

- Ensures Accuracy: Sequentially following each step ensures that you don't miss crucial actions that could affect the outcome, like mixing techniques or ingredient additions.
- Building Confidence: Taking your time with each step helps build confidence, allowing you to focus on mastering each technique without feeling rushed.

- Achieving Desired Results: Properly following the sequence helps achieve the desired texture, flavor, and appearance in your baked goods.

Attention to Detail:

- Oven Temperature: Accurate oven temperature is vital for proper baking. Preheat your oven as instructed and use an oven thermometer to ensure it reaches the correct temperature.
- Mixing Techniques: Different recipes require different mixing methods, such as folding or creaming. Understanding and applying these correctly can influence the texture and structure of your baked goods.
- Ingredient Order: Ingredients are often listed in the order they should be added. Following this order helps ensure proper mixing and activation of ingredients like leaveners.

Tips for Managing Time Effectively:

- Prepare in Advance: Pre-measure ingredients and set up all necessary tools before starting. This preparation helps streamline the process and reduces stress.
- Set Timers: Use timers for each stage of the baking process to keep track of time accurately, whether for baking, resting, or cooling periods.

Troubleshooting Common Issues:

- Over-baked Goods: If your baked items come out too dry or overdone, double-check oven temperatures and baking times. Make adjustments as needed based on your oven's calibration.
- Dense Texture: If a recipe results in a dense product, review your mixing techniques and ingredient measurements to ensure they were followed correctly.
- Missteps in Sequencing: If you accidentally skip a step, assess whether it's salvageable or if you need to start over. Some mistakes, like adding an ingredient in the wrong order, can often be corrected, while others might require a redo.

By practicing careful recipe reading and execution, you'll develop a deeper understanding of baking mechanics, leading to more successful and satisfying results. Remember, patience and precision are key to mastering the art of baking.

Step 7: Experiment and Enjoy

Once you've mastered basic baking techniques and recipes, it's time to let your creativity shine! Experimenting with different flavors and add-ins can transform a simple recipe into something uniquely yours. This step is all about embracing the joy of baking and letting your imagination guide you.

Encouraging Creativity and Exploration:

1. Discover New Flavors: Start by incorporating simple add-ins like chocolate chips, nuts, or dried fruits into your recipes. These additions can enhance the texture and taste of your baked goods, offering delightful surprises in every bite.
2. Customize Recipes: Feel free to tweak the basic recipes you know and love. Add a hint of cinnamon to your muffins, or a splash of vanilla extract to your cookies. Experimenting with spices like nutmeg or cardamom can also add depth to your creations.
3. Incorporate Seasonal Ingredients: Use fresh, seasonal fruits like berries in summer or apples in autumn to add freshness and natural sweetness to your recipes. This not only enhances flavor but also aligns your baking with what's available locally.

Emphasizing Fun and Enjoyment:

- Baking as a Creative Outlet: Let baking become a form of self-expression. Whether you're crafting cookies with unexpected combinations or designing a cake with your favorite toppings, the process should be enjoyable and fulfilling.
- Relax and Play: Don't stress over perfection. Allow yourself to play with ingredients and enjoy the act of baking. Remember, the goal is to have fun and explore new possibilities.

Tips for Safe Experimentation:

- *Start Small*: Test new ideas with a small batch. This way, if the experiment doesn't go as planned, you haven't used up all your ingredients.
- *Balance Flavors*: When trying new combinations, think about how the flavors might complement or contrast each other. A little trial and error will help you find the perfect balance.
- *Keep Notes*: Document your experiments, noting what worked and what didn't. This will be invaluable as you refine your techniques and develop your signature recipes.

Learning from Mistakes:

- *Embrace Imperfection*: Mistakes are a natural part of the learning process. Each one is an opportunity to learn and improve your skills.
- *Reflect and Adjust*: If something doesn't turn out as expected, analyze what might have gone wrong and how you can adjust next time. This reflection will improve your understanding and confidence.

Building Confidence and Skills:

- *Celebrate Successes*: No matter how small, celebrate your successes. Each successful experiment builds your confidence and inspires you to try more.

- ***Expand Your Repertoire***: As you become more comfortable with experimentation, gradually introduce more complex techniques and ingredients. This will expand your baking repertoire and skill set.

By embracing experimentation and enjoying the baking process, you open yourself to a world of culinary possibilities. Let each baking session be a joyful journey of discovery, creativity, and learning.

Conclusion

Thank you for journeying through this guide on sourdough discard recipes. Your commitment to exploring the world of sourdough discard marks the beginning of a rewarding baking adventure. Sourdough discard, often underestimated, is a treasure trove of flavors and possibilities just waiting to enhance your culinary creations. By utilizing this often-overlooked ingredient, you not only embrace a sustainable baking practice but also enrich your kitchen repertoire with a host of delightful recipes.

As you've seen, sourdough discard transforms ordinary dishes into extraordinary ones with its unique tang and depth. From pancakes and waffles to cookies and crackers, the range of recipes you can explore is vast. This guide was designed to inspire you to make the most out of every ingredient, turning potential waste into something wonderful and delicious.

Using sourdough discard in your recipes offers several benefits. Its natural fermentation process not only adds a distinct flavor but also aids digestion, lowers the glycemic index, and enhances nutrient bioavailability. These health benefits, coupled with the sheer joy of baking, make sourdough discard an invaluable addition to your kitchen.

Now, with these insights, it's time to take your newfound knowledge and continue your exploration. The beauty of sourdough discard lies in its versatility. Feel free to experiment with flavors and textures—add spices, nuts, fruits, or whatever excites your palate. Each variation offers a new opportunity to discover something delightful.

Share your creations with friends and family. Invite them to partake in your culinary experiments and gather their feedback. Baking is a communal activity, bringing people together through shared experiences and flavors. The joy of watching others enjoy your creations is unparalleled and can provide inspiration for your next baking endeavor.

Document your experiments, both successes and challenges. Keeping a journal or notebook can help track what worked and what didn't, serving as a personal guidebook for future recipes. Over time, this collection of notes will become a treasure trove of personalized recipes and experiences.

Every baker faces challenges, so don't let occasional mishaps discourage you. Each mistake presents a valuable opportunity to learn and refine your skills, deepening your understanding of ingredients and techniques. The journey of baking with sourdough discard is as rewarding as the final creation itself.

Embrace the joy of experimentation and take pride in crafting something that is uniquely yours.

As you delve deeper into the art of baking, consider exploring the broader spectrum of sourdough. The complexity and richness of sourdough bread itself offer another layer of culinary exploration. You might find joy in experimenting with different grains, fermentation times, and hydration levels to craft your perfect loaf.

The kitchen is your canvas, and sourdough discard is your palette. Whether you're refining a classic recipe or embarking on a new culinary journey, approach each baking session with curiosity and joy. The aromas, textures, and flavors that emerge from your kitchen are a testament to your creativity and passion.

Thank you for taking the time to explore sourdough discard baking. Your willingness to learn and experiment is at the heart of what makes this culinary journey so rewarding. As you continue to embody the artistry and science of baking, may each creation bring joy to your table and those around you. Embrace the endless possibilities and let sourdough discard be your guide to delicious new adventures.

FAQs

What is sourdough discard, and how is it different from an active starter?

Sourdough discard is the portion of the sourdough starter that is removed during the feeding process. Unlike an active starter, which is bubbly and ready for bread-making, discard is less active but still contains wild yeast and bacteria. It's perfect for recipes that do not require strong leavening but benefit from the tangy flavor and nutritional benefits it offers.

Can sourdough discard be used immediately after removing it from the starter?

Yes, sourdough discard can be used immediately in recipes. However, if you plan to store it for later use, keep it in a sealed container in the refrigerator for up to a week. This slows down fermentation, keeping it usable for a variety of recipes.

What are some health benefits of using sourdough discard in recipes?

Sourdough discard offers several health benefits due to its natural fermentation process. It can aid digestion, lower the glycemic index of baked goods, and increase the bioavailability of nutrients. This makes it a nutritious addition to your recipes, providing both flavor and health benefits.

How can I adjust recipes to include sourdough discard?

When incorporating sourdough discard, you may need to adjust the liquid and flour ratios in your recipes. Typically, the discard can replace an equivalent amount of liquid and a small amount of flour. Start with recipes that naturally accommodate extra liquid, like pancakes or muffins, and experiment gradually.

Can I freeze sourdough discard for future use?

Yes, you can freeze sourdough discard. Place it in an airtight container or a freezer bag, and it will keep for several months. Thaw it in the refrigerator before using it in recipes, and give it a good stir to ensure even distribution of its natural cultures.

What types of recipes are best suited for sourdough discard?

Sourdough discard is versatile and can be used in a variety of recipes such as pancakes, waffles, muffins, crackers, and even pizza dough. Its tangy flavor adds depth to both sweet and savory dishes, making it a wonderful addition to many baked goods.

How can I ensure my sourdough discard doesn't spoil before I use it?

To prevent spoilage, store sourdough discard in a sealed container in the refrigerator. Use it within a week for optimal flavor and freshness. If you notice an off smell, mold, or unusual color, it's best to discard it and start fresh. Keeping it properly stored and using it promptly will help maintain its quality.

References and Helpful Links

Anastopoulo, R. (2024, April 18). What is sourdough discard? And what should I do with it? King Arthur Baking. https://www.kingarthurbaking.com/blog/2024/04/18/sourdough-discard#:~:text=Sourdough%20discard%20is%20the%20portion,it%20or%20bake%20with%20it.

Bass, L. (2024, May 8). 15+ healthy sourdough discard recipes. Farmhouse on Boone. https://www.farmhouseonboone.com/15-healthy-sourdough-discard-recipes/#:~:text=The%20best%20part%20about%20using,better%20absorbed%20by%20the%20body.

Mama, P. (2023, November 15). Sourdough Starter vs Sourdough Discard: What's The Difference? - The Pantry Mama. The Pantry Mama. https://www.pantrymama.com/sourdough-starter-vs-sourdough-discard/

Heather. (2021, November 15). Ultimate Guide To Sourdough Discard (Tips, FAQ's, and Recipes!). Boston Girl Bakes. https://www.bostongirlbakes.com/ultimate-guide-to-sourdough-discard-tips-faqs-and-recipes/

Countryroadssourdough. (2024, February 19). Sourdough Discard: Everything you Need to Know. Country Roads Sourdough. https://countryroadssourdough.com/sourdough-discard/

Mama, P. (2023a, February 23). How to add sourdough discard to any recipe - The pantry mama. The Pantry Mama. https://www.pantrymama.com/how-to-add-sourdough-discard-to-any-recipe/

Leisha. (2024, June 3). Can you freeze sourdough discard for later use? Lockrem Homestead. https://lockremhomestead.com/2024/03/25/can-you-freeze-sourdough-discard-for-later-use/

www.ingramcontent.com/pod-product-compliance
Lightning Source LLC
LaVergne TN
LVHW012030060526
838201LV00061B/4540